TONY STEWART
DRIVEN TO WIN

TRIUMPH
BOOKS
CHICAGO

Author:
Jason Mitchell

Photography:
The Charlotte Observer

Editor:
Constance Holloway

Design Team:
Larry Preslar
Beth Epperly
Andrea Ross

This book is a joint production of
Triumph Books and the New Ventures
Division of Knight Publishing Co.

This book is not sponsored, authorized
or endorsed by or otherwise affiliated
with NASCAR or any person featured
within this book. This is not an official
publication.

This book is available in quantity at
special discounts for your group or
organization. For further information,
contact:

Triumph Books
601 South LaSalle Street, Suite 500
Chicago, Illinois 60605
(312) 939-3330
Fax (312) 663-3557

Printed in the United States of America

ISBN 1-57243-553-4

Jason Mitchell is a veteran NASCAR Winston Cup Series freelance writer who resides in Concord, North Carolina.

Mitchell was born August 14, 1972 in Fort Walton Beach, Florida. While he was young, Mitchell's family moved to North Wilkesboro, North Carolina. His love for auto racing began while growing up around the now-defunct North Wilkesboro Speedway, which until 1996 hosted two NASCAR Winston Cup Series races a year.

Mitchell graduated from Appalachian State University in Boone, North Carolina in 1996 with a bachelor of science degree in communications. He majored in public relations with a minor in marketing.

Upon graduation, Mitchell became assistant sports editor at the *Wilkes Journal-Patriot.* Trying to get closer to the "hub" of racing in and around Charlotte, North Carolina, Mitchell moved and spent four years as the motorsports writer with the *Independent Tribune* in Concord.

Mitchell's freelance writing has been included in *Stock Car Racing* magazine, *NASCAR Magazine, Inside NASCAR, Racing Milestones, Last Lap,* as well as program work for Lowe's Motor Speedway and International Speedway Corporation. Some of Mitchell's technical writing has appeared on NASCAR.com.

TONY STEWART

Stats

Cars:
No. 20 Home Depot Chevrolet

Major Wins:
15 (Winston Cup), 3 (IRL)

Earnings:
$21.4 million

Poles:
6 (Winston Cup), 9 (IRL)

Top 5 Finishes:
54

Top 10 Finishes:
87

Championships:
- 2002 NASCAR Winston Cup Series
- 1999 Rookie of the Year
- 1997 Indy Racing League

Teams:
Joe Gibbs Racing (Winston),
Team Menard (IRL)

Sponsors:
Home Depot, Chevrolet, Old Spice, Coca-Cola,
Champion, Goodyear, MBNA, Phillips

Unique Facts:
Raced in the Indy 500 and Coca-Cola 600 in the same day.

TABLE OF CONTENTS

a passionate RACER

1

When it comes to NASCAR Winston Cup Series competitor Tony Stewart, most race fans come down on one side of the fence or the other about the driver of the No. 20 Home Depot Chevrolet.

It's clear each racing weekend when Stewart's name is announced during driver introductions. He draws a response of some sort from everybody in the grandstands, be it good or bad. Some fans love his win-at-all-cost attitude while others could do without it. Whether you like him or not, Stewart has earned respect with 14 victories and counting in only four short seasons on the Winston Cup tour. Many felt that 2002 would be the year that Stewart scored the first of several Winston Cup titles in what should be a bright career.

The late Dale Earnhardt once joked that if the fans weren't applauding or booing, the driver wasn't doing his job. Stewart is very much cut from that same mold, as he too seems to feed off his critics. Stewart has been called volatile, but so too have some of the greatest drivers in NASCAR history. If having a burning desire to win races and contend for championships is a crime, Stewart pleads guilty as charged.

"Being volatile doesn't make you a good driver," Stewart explains. "Winning races makes you a good driver. The distractions outside of the car are what make me volatile, so I'm eliminating the distractions and probably won't be volatile this year."

Volatility is the very reason that Stewart has become so popular because racing fans are tired of drivers getting out of their cars after a bad day and saying things that are politically correct. If

If having a burning desire to win races and contend for championships is a crime, Stewart pleads guilty as charged.

Stewart is asked what's on his mind, he will give an honest answer with little regard for saying the right thing.

However, saying what's on his mind has led to several problems off the track. One of Stewart's main problems has been dealing with some members of the motorsports media. Before the 2002 season started, Stewart vowed that would change.

"If it doesn't make the car go faster or doesn't promote Home Depot, I'm not doing it," Stewart said. "I'm not messing with it. I'm not messing with the outside distractions. I'll show you my contract. In my contract, it tells me what I have to do and what I don't have to do."

Stewart also has a simple request for the media: a cooling-off period that is commonplace for athletes in other professional sports.

"My challenge to the media is to give me 15 minutes of cooldown time after a race," Stewart said. "If they give me that courtesy this year, I will give them what they need to get their job done. It's a two-way street. If the media works with me, then I will work with them. If it's a distraction of what I'm trying to do, I'm going to cut it off. My job is to drive, and if any of it is a distraction to what I'm doing in the race car, it's going to be cut it off. There are a lot of people that have always known how to handle it. It's just that everybody [in the media] is learning this deal and how to work with us in the garage. Once everybody figures that out, I think everybody will be happy with the results they get."

After several highly publicized tirades throughout his young career, Stewart has visibly taken a more mature approach in dealing with adversity.

The competitive fire remains, but Stewart has learned that sometimes it's better to say nothing than to make remarks that could hurt the image of his sponsors and NASCAR.

Yet many of Stewart's fans like him not only for his driving skill, but also for having the guts to speak his mind when he feels like he's been wronged. Stewart believes the fans deserve candid answers. In all honesty, Stewart is simply saying things that all drivers feel the same way about but are too scared to say.

"I believe the people who read what the media writes and prints deserve an honest answer to honest questions," Stewart said. "That's the way my stand has been up to this point, and it's always going to be that way. I'm not doing my job if I don't give honest answers."

Stewart is not above saying there have been some things he's done that he would like to take back while he learned the ropes at the Winston Cup level.

"I've learned a big lesson in life," Stewart said. "I thought that once I got to this level, I'd have everything I wanted. I thought I'd be as happy as I could ever be. And at times, I have been happier than I ever thought I could be. But there have been times in the last year and a half when I have been more miserable than I have ever been.

"When I signed up with Joe Gibbs to come run Winston Cup, I thought I understood everything that was going to happen. Now I realize I knew so little about what was going to change in my life over a very short amount of time. I stay away from controversy now. I don't care if it's about the weather or whatever you want to complain about. I'm out of it. I'm just happy to not be a part of controversy anymore."

the road to STARDOM

To say that Tony Stewart's rise through the various ranks of motorsports has been phenomenal would be an understatement. It all started as a dream when Stewart was growing up in his hometown of Rushville, Indiana.

From a young age, Stewart was exposed to racing due in large part to his living about an hour from the legendary Indianapolis Motor Speedway.

To this day, Stewart still says his favorite driver of all time is A. J. Foyt, who drove to fame in the open-wheel ranks. Since his early exposure to Indy Car racing, many thought a career in that series would be a natural.

In 1983, Stewart became a champion in the International Karting Foundation's Grand National division. Four years later,

he earned the World Karting Association's national championship.

As Stewart ascended the racing ladder, many team owners began taking notice of his natural talent. It was in 1991 when Stewart tried his hand in the USAC (United States Auto Club) open-wheel ranks, winning Sprint Car Rookie-of-the-Year honors. He competed in several divisions that year, doing well in every type of car he drove. Stewart also picked up the Rookie-of-the-Year award by finishing an impressive fifth in the points race at Indianapolis Speedrome in the Midget Series. He also picked up his first USAC Midget victory on August 9, 1991 at the Speedrome.

After learning the ropes at the USAC level, Stewart reached stardom in

As Stewart ascended the racing ladder, many team owners began taking notice of his natural talent.

1994 when he won the national Midget championship thanks to five victories. At the time, he was still trying his hand at the more powerful Sprint division, posting a runner-up finish in the famous USAC Silver Crown's Copper World Classic at Phoenix.

In 1995, Stewart became the first and only driver in USAC history to win the sport's "Triple Crown" of titles. He captured championships in the National Midget, Sprint, and Silver Crown divisions.

Stewart's lifelong dream of racing in the Indianapolis 500 was realized in 1996 when he moved up to the Indy Racing League. He made his debut at Indianapolis in convincing fashion by winning the pole at a speed of 235.837 mph

around the legendary 2.5-mile track. Stewart led 43 laps of the race before falling short of the victory. He ended the season with an eighth-place finish in the final IRL point standings. In addition to his IRL efforts, Stewart had started to feel the lure of NASCAR stock cars and ran eight races in the Busch Series for Ranier/Walsh Racing.

According to Stewart, one of the defining moments of his career came when NASCAR team owner Joe Gibbs offered him the opportunity to drive his Busch Series car on a limited basis in 1997. In addition to his Busch Series efforts, Stewart also competed full-time in the IRL and won the 1997 series championship.

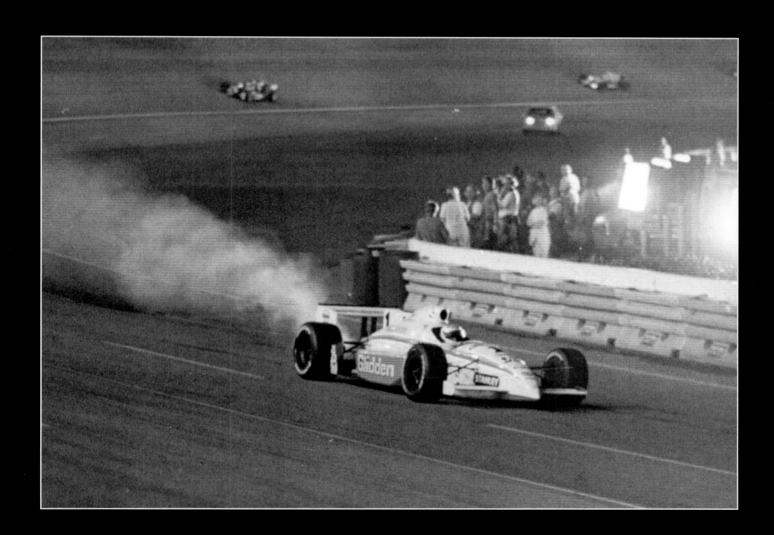

In 1998, Stewart shifted his focus to Gibbs' Busch Series program and ran 22 races while completing another full season in the IRL. With his NASCAR efforts, Stewart won two poles and posted five top-five finishes. In the IRL, Stewart won two races and four poles while finishing third in the point standings.

Gibbs, a retired NFL head football coach, wanted a talented young driver to add to his racing stable as a teammate to Bobby Labonte for the 1999 season. His decision to move Stewart up into the NASCAR Winston Cup Series would make the former Super Bowl-winning coach look like a genius in another very different form of competition.

Not since Jeff Gordon broke into the Winston Cup scene in 1993 had a rookie excelled as Stewart did in his first season at NASCAR's premier level. While Gordon's rookie season was good, Stewart's was nothing short of incredible as "The Rushville Rocket" won three races and finished fourth in the final standings. Stewart easily won the Winston Cup Rookie-of-the-Year award. Stewart's success also seemed to spill over to the No. 18 team of Labonte as he won a career-best five victories a year before winning the Winston Cup championship in 2000.

Showing his first season wasn't a fluke, Stewart won six races in 2000 and finished sixth in the final standings. The following year, Stewart picked up three wins before finishing second in the points race behind four-time champion Jeff Gordon. An interesting parallel between Stewart and Gordon is that both drivers were raised in Indiana, and many people thought they would end up driving Indy-style cars. But as the 2001 season showed, the two were at the top of their game in NASCAR.

Another interesting note regarding the two is that their success has opened doors for other young and talented drivers who had historically been told that it takes the skill of a veteran to get the job done. Even though Stewart and Gordon never experienced a great deal of success in the Busch Series, they have asserted themselves as proven commodities at the Winston Cup level.

Stewart might not have traveled the usual road to reach the pinnacle of Winston Cup racing, but his natural driving talent will keep him in winning contention for many years.

3

ROOKIE
phenomenon

The successful Winston Cup career of Tony Stewart really can't be traced to one race, due in large part to the success of his rookie season. At tracks he had never seen before, Stewart set rookie records with three wins and an incredible fourth-place finish in the final 1999 point standings.

By winning Rookie-of-the Year honors, Stewart joined an elite class of drivers that includes Richard Petty, David Pearson, Ricky Rudd, Dale Earnhardt, Rusty Wallace, Alan Kulwicki, Davey Allison, Jeff Gordon, and Jeff Burton. Among this all-star cast of drivers, Stewart's overall first-year results were better than anyone else's.

As a reward for his efforts, Stewart earned almost $3.2 million. What many people didn't know about Stewart is that he could honestly care less about the money. For him, the chance to win wakes him up every morning.

Ignoring the "sophomore jinx," Stewart rebounded from a sluggish start to the 2000 season with six more victories. Due to not finishing five races that year, Stewart would end up sixth in the points while his Joe Gibbs Racing teammate, Bobby Labonte, won the Winston Cup title.

In 2001, Stewart finished a career-best second in the Winston Cup Series championship with only two victories. More important than putting up numbers in the win column, Stewart was racing with the consistency needed to contend for a championship. He would post 15 top-five finishes throughout the course of the 2001 season, along with seven top-10 efforts. During the course of the year, Stewart would also win the Bud

Ignoring the "sophomore jinx," Tony Stewart rebounded from a sluggish start to the 2000 season with six more victories. Due to not finishing five races that year, Stewart would end up sixth in the points while his Joe Gibbs Racing teammate, Bobby Labonte, won the Winston Cup title.

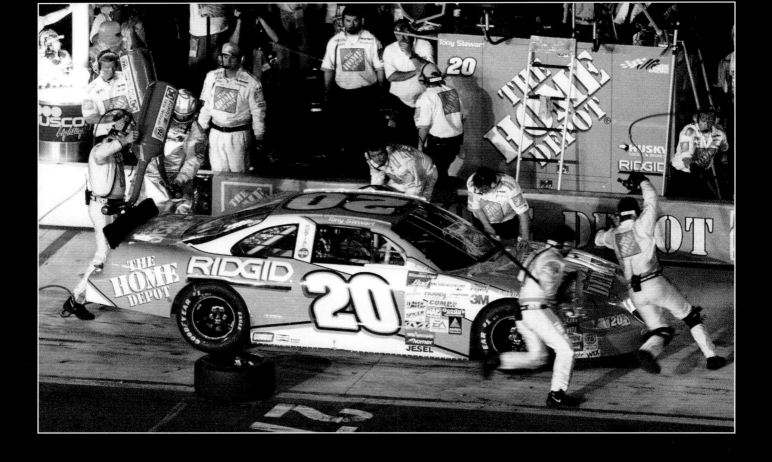

"There's always going to be a lot of talent coming into Winston Cup racing," said Tony Stewart. "This is the best racing series in the country, if not the world, and this is where everybody wants to be. Every place else people are at right now, they're using as a stepping-stone into Winston Cup. You're going to get the best of the best."

Shootout in Daytona and pick up his first victory in an International Race of Champions event at Michigan.

Stewart admits his early success has him in awe of all he's accomplished so quickly.

"To be able to do what we've done in such a short period of time, I feel like I've hit the lottery," Stewart says. "Not many people in this garage area have had the opportunity that I've had. If you take the point standings aside and just look at our seasons in 2000 and 2001, 2000 was just a much better year than 2001 was, in my opinion. We finished sixth in points that year and we won six races. Last year we finished second in a season that we felt was worse. That is what was so surprising. It just shows that there's no blueprint of what it takes to be a Winston Cup champion."

In his three seasons, Stewart has seen three drivers—Dale Jarrett, Labonte, and Gordon—win the Winston Cup championship. He has watched and patiently learned from those drivers to see what it takes to pull off the feat. Stewart knows it's a goal that he can reach, but he's also very aware that it is going to take a nearly flawless season to earn the title.

"In our hearts and our minds, we want to win the championship, but being the realists that we are, we're just worried about being consistent," Stewart says. "If we as a team can go out there and give it 110 percent each week, taking it one race at a time and doing the best job we can, then where we are at the end of the year is where we're going to be. As long as we know in our hearts that we gave it all we had each week, that's all we can do.

"We can only control the variables that we're in control of."

There are so many variables that we're not in control of. We can't just sit here and say we want to win the championship this year because we finished second last year and anything less than that will be disappointing. That's a foolish attitude to take so early in the season."

The numbers Stewart has put up on the board in three full seasons is nothing short of remarkable.

At the start of 2002, Stewart went into the Daytona 500 with 12 victories, four poles, 40 top-five finishes, and 60 top 10s.

In a season dominated by young competitors, Stewart knew that with the likes of Dale Earnhardt Jr., Matt Kenseth, Kurt Busch, Jimmie Johnson, and Ryan Newman winning races on a regular basis, victories would be harder to come by.

"I have the utmost respect for those guys," Stewart said of the sport's newcomers. "I ran against them in the Busch Series and I know what they're capable of. If you look at my career in that series and what I have done in Winston Cup, and then look at what those guys have done in the Busch Series, you can only imagine what they're going to do.

"There's always going to be a lot of talent coming into Winston Cup racing. This is the best racing series in the country, if not the world, and this is where everybody wants to be. Every place else people are at right now, they're using as a stepping-stone into Winston Cup. You're going to get the best of the best."

In his three seasons, Stewart has seen three drivers—Dale Jarrett, Bobby Labonte, and Jeff Gordon—win the Winston Cup championship. He has watched and patiently learned from those drivers to see what it takes to pull off the feat. Stewart knows it's a goal that he can reach, but he's also very aware that it is going to take a nearly flawless season to earn the title.

4

SHINING
career moments

Just seven days after Tony Stewart outdueled "The Intimidator," Dale Earnhardt was killed in a last-lap crash in the Daytona 500.

Tony Stewart remembers the greatest Winston Cup Series victory of his career not because of the track he was on or the stature of the race. He remembers it for the driver he beat in the closing laps to score the win.

Following his victory in 2001's night race at Bristol Motor Speedway, Stewart was asked if that win was the biggest of his career. Stewart thought about the question for a moment before his thoughts returned to the 2001 Budweiser Shootout at Daytona International Speedway, when he held off seven-time Winston Cup champion Dale Earnhardt, who was driving his legendary black No. 3 Chevrolet.

"Bristol is one of the most satisfying, but I don't think it's the biggest," Stewart explained. "I still think the biggest is beating Dale Earnhardt in the Shootout. It was more of a personal triumph for me

than anything. It was cool the day that I won at Daytona. It was intimidating for me to see him back there, but at the same time I had to do my job. You know he had more tricks in his book than anybody else. Then after we lost Dale, it made it even more special."

Only seven days after Stewart outdueled "The Intimidator," Earnhardt was killed in a last-lap crash in the Daytona 500.

Stewart says another of his most special wins came earlier in 2002 at Atlanta when he scored the victory in the NMBA 500 after another challenge from the Earnhardt racing family in the form of Dale Earnhardt Jr., who finished second.

"I would have sworn that car behind me was black and had a No. 3 on it because Dale Jr. may have 'Jr.' behind his name, but he drives like Dale Earnhardt Sr.," Stewart said following the race. "He's

got all the talent in the world. He's got all the talent that his dad had. It was an honor to race with him. I knew it was going to be Dale Jr. and me at the end. I knew he'd help me get to the front, because I'd helped him get to the front. But in the end, we both knew it was every man for himself."

The Atlanta victory also marked Stewart's first Winston Cup win in a 500-mile race.

"Finally, it's been a long time coming," Stewart said following the 13th win of his career. "The first thing I thought of when we crossed the finish line is that I finally won a 500-mile race. I don't know why we haven't won one before now. It just seems like the races that we really run well at are 400-mile races or shorter. It was nice to finally get one and it gives me a lot of confidence."

Of course, the chance to go to victory lane and be called a winner at the Winston Cup level is something drivers always hold special. Stewart had picked up his first victory in NASCAR's premier division in fall 1999 by leading 333 laps before winning the Exide 400 at Richmond International Raceway.

For the first time in his career, Stewart was literally speechless over winning in only his 25th Winston Cup career start.

"I wish I knew what to say," Stewart said after climbing out of his car. "You plan all your life for this. I think this is the first time I have been speechless. We've been shooting for it all year."

As if to make sure everybody knew his Richmond victory wasn't a fluke, Stewart completed a wildly successful season with back-to-back victories at Phoenix and Homestead-Miami. Those wins allowed Stewart to become the first rookie in Winston Cup history to win three races. Stewart won a pair of poles in 1999 and 2000, but was shut out in 2001.

Stewart says one of his most surprising wins came in 2001 when he won at the Sears Point road course.

According to Stewart, road racing was not a part of his upbringing. He had won at every kind of racing he had ever run in, but he spent two years learning how to sling a road-racing car right instead of the standard left-handers.

"I never ran a road course other than go-karts," he said. "I would say getting our first win in our fifth road-course race is pretty good."

Stewart has won at virtually every type of track on the Winston Cup tour.

While the Budweiser Shootout is a special nonpoints race, Stewart has proven he can win on the high banks of Daytona. His ace in the hole seems to be short tracks, where he's earned three victories at Richmond along with wins at Martinsville and Bristol. Stewart also seems to excel on flat race tracks as evident by wins at Homestead, Michigan, New Hampshire, and Phoenix.

While Stewart is only in his fourth season at the Winston Cup level, he has proven to be a threat to win every time he gets behind the wheel.

TONY'S *Temper*

Losing is something that Tony Stewart really hates. He feels like losing is a slap in the face. If he didn't feel that passion, he says, he would look for another job outside of racing.

Unfortunately for Stewart, much of the attention he has gained has been because of what some consider to be his bad temper. Those fans don't get the chance to see that Stewart is a genuinely good person, instead focusing on some of his past temper tantrums.

One of the first times Stewart showed his emotional and passionate side was at Martinsville Speedway when he and Kenny Irwin got into a bumping match with their cars. Stewart would end up getting the worst end of the stick as Irwin spun him entering the first turn at the Virginia short track. After his car came to a rest, Stewart climbed out and

waited for Irwin's machine to come back around. Stewart wound up literally trying to jump into Irwin's car in retaliation.

Following Irwin's fatal 2000 crash at New Hampshire International Speedway, Stewart later commented that his action at Martinsville was something he deeply regretted. By looking into his eyes when talking about Irwin, it is apparent that he is sincere. Irwin and Stewart cut their racing teeth together in the open-wheel ranks, and both had made it at the Winston Cup level. They were both equally as passionate about the sport.

"There are 43 guys that start the race every week and you're not going to get along with all of them 100 percent of the time," Stewart said.

Another of Stewart's high-profile blowups happened after a practice crash with Robby Gordon in preparation for

The goal for team owner Joe Gibbs has been to get Tony Stewart to channel his emotions in a positive way instead of getting into repeated trouble with the sanctioning body.

the 2000 Daytona 500. In the moments that followed, a heated confrontation erupted between the two before they were separated in the Daytona garage area. One of the most entertaining moments of Stewart's career came in the 2001 spring race at Bristol when Jeff Gordon bumped him out of the way for position on the final lap.

An angry Stewart retaliated by spinning Gordon's car out as he was coming down pit road afterward.

Gordon insisted it was just a racing incident but joked that he wasn't at all shocked to get bumped back.

"That didn't surprise me one bit," Gordon said at the time. "I didn't want it to come to the last lap like that, but if you've got a position and you've been working on it for a long time, you're going to do it and you're going to take everything you can all the way to the end. I thought it was pretty clean."

For his actions, Stewart was fined $10,000 and placed on probation. Later that same season, controversy again found Stewart when he ignored a black flag over a disputed on-track rule infraction in the July race at Daytona. Stewart finished the race without acknowledging the penalty, and afterward got into a heated confrontation with NASCAR official Gary Nelson and a member of the motorsports media. As a result, Stewart was again slapped with a $10,000 fine and had his probation extended through the end of the 2001 season.

Stewart acknowledged some of his actions, though he still felt the penalty was wrong.

"While I disagree with the black flag penalty, I accept the fine and probation that NASCAR has issued to me as a result of my post-race conduct," Stewart said. "My behavior was inappropriate, and for that I apologize. For others I may have offended, I regret that also. I will continue to work with all those people who support me on handling these types of situations better in the future."

Many insiders thought Stewart got off too lightly while others thought he might be briefly suspended. Stewart has matured a great deal since that warm July night in Daytona, and admits one of the reasons he's been able to stay out of

controversy is his talks with team owner Joe Gibbs.

Gibbs compared Stewart to some of the football players he'd coached along the way. Some were emotional while others were more low key. The goal for Gibbs has been to get Stewart to channel his emotions in a positive way instead of getting into repeated trouble with the sanctioning body.

"Tony is very emotional, driven to win, explodes, but that's his personality," Gibbs said. "Over time he will be able to control that, I hope. When you're dealing with different athletes and different guys, people deal with things in different ways. I can be part of the blame here, because as I've tried to work through this thing with Tony, I told him, 'When you're upset like that after a race, the best thing to do is just go to the motor home.'

"Having said that, there have been times when the media's gotten upset with him because he wouldn't talk to them. But I try to tell all my guys that in professional sports, it's not a perfect world.

And everybody's different, including Tony. I don't want him to change his personality, but just be more cautious at times."

Stewart is the first to admit there are things that, over time, he will hopefully be more capable of controlling.

"There's been so many things that have happened," Stewart said. "I feel like I've done everything that I've needed to do, or in all reality, at least what I thought I should be doing. Some things I haven't done the right way, and those things I would do different. There's a whole list of things that I should have done different, but you learn as you go. When you get your NASCAR license, there isn't a manual that they give you on how to live your life as a Winston Cup driver. I'm just going a chapter at a time."

6

gibbs takes A GAMBLE

In 1999, team owner Joe Gibbs added Tony Stewart as a teammate to Bobby Labonte. As his three-win rookie season proved, Gibbs had another winning team on his hands with Stewart and crew chief Greg Zipadelli.

Through his many years of advancing through the ranks, Tony Stewart was well aware of the importance of having a good race team behind him. That's what made it such an easy choice when Joe Gibbs approached Stewart to talk about the possibility of moving him up to the Winston Cup Series.

It was the realization of a lifelong dream to get the chance at NASCAR's top level. Stewart credits two people who have played a major role in his Winston Cup career. One of those is Gibbs, who gave him the opportunity to show his talent; the other is crew chief Greg Zipadelli.

While Gibbs often stays busy overseeing his race teams and other business ventures, Stewart and Zipadelli have

grown to be close friends through the good times and the bad.

If you think Stewart is driven to succeed, Zipadelli is cut from the same mold thanks to his past championship crew chief experience in the Busch North and Featherlite Modified ranks.

"I think in a lot of ways I'm a carbon copy of Tony," said Zipadelli, who is also noted for not being afraid to speak his mind. "I've just learned to control my emotions and not show them on the outside. I'm one of those people that will hold everything in. I probably get as mad or frustrated with a lot of things, but at the same time it's my job as a leader of the other 17 or 18 people that stand in the pits and support the car and driver. If I don't do those things, then I'm not

setting a good example for the rest of my people on how they need to act.

"It's a requirement in this sport today. It's just the way things are going. I look at it and take it as my responsibility to accept these things and do the best I can with them. Sometimes it's hard, but I think I've been doing a good job at it."

If you're a Joe Gibbs employee, success is expected.

Before entering racing, Gibbs had already attained fame and glory by leading the NFL's Washington Redskins to three Super Bowls. There was always an interest in racing for Gibbs, thanks in large part to his having grown up in North Carolina.

When he decided to enter NASCAR, Gibbs wanted a winner and took a chance on an unproven driver by

the name of Dale Jarrett to start the 1992 season. The chance paid off as the pairing won the 1993 Daytona 500. While Jarrett would drive for Gibbs for three years, he left following the 1994 season to take a ride with Robert Yates.

Again taking a chance on an unproven commodity with talent, Gibbs replaced Jarrett with Bobby Labonte in 1995 and won three races the first year.

While Jarrett would eventually go on to win the title in 1999 with Yates, Gibbs was vindicated in 2000 when Labonte won the Winston Cup championship.

In 1999, Gibbs added Stewart as a teammate to Labonte.

As his three-win rookie season proved, Gibbs had another winning team on his hands with Stewart and Zipadelli.

While other teams approached Stewart with offers of more money, he made his commitment to Gibbs crystal clear.

"You win three races in your rookie season, why would you go anywhere else?" he asked. "It's not all about money. I'd much rather take a smaller paycheck and win races then take a bigger paycheck and run in the back. We're pretty much married to each other now."

For some reason, everyone Gibbs touches turns into a winner.

"You've got to pick the right people to come on your team and try to understand what makes them tick," Gibbs said. "And then how do you get them to accomplish a common goal and sacrifice their own goals? The reason that is so hard is it goes against human nature."

TONY STEWART

career highlights

1995:

Became only driver in history to win the United States Auto (USAC) Club's version of the "Triple Crown" by winning championships in the National Midget, Sprint, and Silver Crown divisions.

1996:

Won the pole for the Indianapolis 500

1997:

Indy Racing League season championship

1998:

Competed in 22 NASCAR Busch Grand National races, winning two poles along with accumulating five top-five and five top-10 finishes.

Also competed in the IRL division, finishing third in the final standings thanks to two victories and four poles.

1999:

Became the first driver in NASCAR Winston Cup Series history to win three races his rookie season driving for Joe Gibbs Racing in the No. 20 Home Depot Pontiac. First career victory came at Richmond on September 11, 1999. Finished fourth in the final point standings while earning Winston Cup Rookie-of-the-Year honors. Competed in the Indianapolis 500 and the Coca-Cola 600 on the same day, completing all but 10 of a possible 1,100 miles. Finished fourth at Charlotte and ninth at Indianapolis. He also won two Winston Cup poles. Stewart's other two victories came at Phoenix and Homestead-Miami.

2000:

Showing his rookie season wasn't a fluke, Stewart won a career-best six races during his sophomore effort. Won two more poles and finished sixth in the final points while watching teammate Bobby Labonte win the Winston Cup championship. Stewart's victories included a sweep of both races at Dover, as well as wins at Michigan, Homestead, New Hampshire, and Martinsville.

2001:

Continuing to improve, Stewart finished a career-best second in the final standings. Started the season by scoring what he considers his greatest victory: beating Dale Earnhardt to win the Budweiser Shootout, only days before the fatal last-lap crash in the Daytona 500 that claimed the life of the seven-time Winston Cup champion. Later in the season Stewart picked up his first road-course win with a daring pass by Robby Gordon and Kevin Harvick.

Also won for the second time in his career at Richmond, before winning the night race at Bristol. Failed to win a pole, but his career earnings in only three full Winston Cup seasons surpassed the $11 million mark.

2002:

In only his fourth season on the tour, Stewart won his first NASCAR Winston Cup Series championship in November at Homestead-Miami Speedway. Stewart beat veteran driver Mark Martin by 38 points in one of the best championship races in Winston Cup history for his first title at NASCAR's top level. Picked up a pair of wins in the first half of the season at Atlanta and Sears Point, backing his drive for the championship up with a victory at Watkins Glen in August. Stewart grabbed the Winston Cup point lead following Talladega in October and never lost the top spot. Stewart enjoyed the best season of his NASCAR career with 15 Top 5 and 21 Top 10 finishes. He also won two poles. Easily the best financial year of Stewart's life with earnings nearing the $5 million mark.

away from THE TRACK

Everybody who works in Winston Cup Series racing loves to take advantage of any free time they have throughout the course of a 36-race schedule that doesn't include non-points races in Daytona and Charlotte.

If Tony Stewart isn't strapped into a Winston Cup stock car, he's likely to be keeping his skills sharp by returning to his Friday and Saturday night racing roots. Stewart is one of NASCAR's most eligible bachelors, but his love for racing takes a backseat to nothing. He remembers telling a girl on a first date that his love of racing could never be replaced by a serious relationship. Stewart wasn't being rude, just stating his usual honest opinion.

Through the years, Stewart's approach to life has become somewhat mellowed with more thoughts on how he wants to

be remembered when he is no longer a part of the Winston Cup picture.

"I don't care if I die a millionaire or with 10 cents in my pocket," Stewart says. "I want to be a good husband some day, and a good father. I also want people to say I was a good person when I die."

At this point in his career, racing is Stewart's true love. Like any single guy, Stewart appreciates the small things in life like a day of splashing around the waters of Lake Norman. If you're lucky and at the right spot around Charlotte, North Carolina, don't be surprised to see Stewart trying his hand at bowling or playing pool at the local billiards hall.

Stewart splits his free time between homes at Lake Norman in North Carolina and Columbus, Indiana.

Of course, being a true racer at heart, if Stewart has the chance to race in any

The World of Outlaws division is a totally different opportunity for Tony Stewart to have a little fun.

kind of competition you might as well count him in.

"I've been in a monster truck, so we can cross that one of the list," Stewart said. "I haven't raced swamp buggies, motorcycles, or drag cars. That's about it. There's not much left."

At this point, many feel Stewart's main goal is to prove he can win the NASCAR Winston Cup Series championship. Honing his racing skills on an "off" Winston Cup weekend certainly isn't out of the ordinary for Stewart. While he has temporarily put a halt to his dreams of winning the Indianapolis 500, Stewart's attempt at winning what he considers the greatest race in the world will never permanently cease.

"Indy is home," Stewart said. "You always want to win and do well at your home track. Knowing the history of the Indianapolis Motor Speedway, the event

is what makes it so big. Driving an Indy car around there for 200 laps is not my idea of a fun day, but having the opportunity to drink the [ceremonial] milk in victory lane is something I dearly hope I have an opportunity to do before I quit driving."

Stewart says the reason he decided to skip the Indianapolis 500 in 2002 was due to his goal of winning the Winston Cup title. Though Indy was placed on the back burner for at least a year, Stewart still enjoyed his open-wheel Indiana roots as a championship team owner for Danny Lasoski in the World of Outlaws division.

"I'll probably have more fun with the series this year than in past years just because I'll be able to watch Danny and see the transitions that he's going to have to make," Stewart said. "I'll enjoy being along there with him so that he can ask me questions and I can give him advice.

I think that's just going to make this year's series a lot of fun."

In terms of being placed in the media spotlight in Winston Cup racing, the World of Outlaws is a totally different opportunity for Stewart to have a little fun.

"It's no pressure for me because I don't drive the cars," Stewart said. "The only pressure for me as a car owner is making sure I give the team the equipment they need to do their jobs properly. Their situation is fairly similar to mine. They run over 100 races a year and there are lots of variables that are out of their control each week.

"So the biggest thing for me is controlling the variables that I can control, and that means giving the team everything they need so that they can go out and do their job to the best of their ability. As long as I do that, it's up to the driver and crew and, of course, a little bit of luck."

racing toward A DREAM

Heading into the summer months of the 2002 season, Tony Stewart was off to a remarkably good start for a driver who was known to perform better as the year wore on. He picked up a pair of wins early in the year at Atlanta and Richmond after suffering a heartbreaking 43rd-place finish in the season-opening Daytona 500 due to a blown engine.

Instead of dwelling on the rough start, Stewart could only look ahead and hope.

"I think everybody is kind of realistic about the fact that with 36 races, any driver is going to have three or four bad days during the year," Stewart said. "You hope you don't have any—but being realistic—everybody expects to have three or four bad races. We just look at Daytona as one of them. You hate to use that card up early, but you know that that is probably going to happen to some of these other people down the road."

Unfortunately, since his first year in Winston Cup racing, playing catch-up in the championship was something Stewart had become accustomed to.

"History has shown that we need to do better the first eight or nine races," Stewart said. "If we can do that and be fairly close to the front, we actually might have a shot at winning a championship. It seems like our weakness is the first eight or nine races."

Instead of struggling early in the 2002 season, Stewart witnessed a dramatic improvement in his consistency. After leaving Daytona a devastating 43rd in the points, Stewart went on a rampage and moved from last to fifth in the standings. That fact had Stewart thinking that 2002 could be the year of his first Winston Cup championship.

"It really excites me knowing that we got off to a good start to the year and

"I think everybody is kind of realistic about the fact that with 36 races, any driver is going to have three or four bad days during the year," Tony Stewart said. "You hope you don't have any— but being realistic—everybody expects to have three or four bad races."

hopefully put ourselves in a position to where we might finally be there at the end of the season," Stewart said. "That right there makes me extremely excited about the possibility of what might lay ahead for us. We've just got to keep our nose to the ground and keep pushing. Hopefully, we'll get there before the end of the year.

"There are so many things that can happen. Do I think we're capable of winning the championship? Absolutely! We've won 12 races in three years and have had four poles, so yeah, we're capable, especially if you look at where we've finished in points the last three years—fourth, sixth, and second. Obviously, we are a contender, but it's just a hard situation to predict. I don't think anyone can honestly and accurately predict what's going to happen and who the contenders

really are until it happens. There's a lot that can happen and a lot of variables can change as time goes on."

Having finished second in 2001's title fight to eventual champion Jeff Gordon, some see a natural rivalry growing between two of the best drivers in Winston Cup racing. Both drivers try to downplay such a rivalry, citing a deep respect for the other's talents.

"It's not a rivalry," Stewart said. "I probably admire Jeff more than I admire anybody in this series by the way he handles everything. He's the kind of guy I look up to and model how I want to make my season work. With 43 guys, it's hard to create an individual rivalry between two guys. A lot of times the media tries to portray a rivalry more than there really is. You've got to remember that we race 38 weekends. We're

with each other 38 weekends a year. It's just like a big, giant family.

"You've got so many people involved that eventually you're going to disagree with somebody along the line. But the next week, you kind of hit a reset button and start all over. That same person you had a problem with the week before may be the guy that helps you or you help him out the next week."

Gordon has admitted that despite his past differences with Stewart, he sees a driver as driven to succeed as he is.

"To me, what stirs up a rivalry is the fans," Gordon said. "Anybody who is competitive week in and week out and makes you battle them for the championship, that to me is your stiffest competition. I don't like the word rivalry. If Tony and me continue to run well like we have in the past, I'm sure we're going to have

some more battles, but that doesn't mean we have to bump and bang and all that. We are two very competitive people who want to run good and finish good."

Make no mistake about Tony Stewart, he is a man driven to succeed. Losing is not something he takes easily.

As it stands now, Stewart longs to become the best of the best and win the Winston Cup championship.

"I don't care about the money," Stewart said. "All I care about is putting trophies on my shelf and winning championships. I'm very passionate in what I do. This is what I've dedicated my whole life to doing and I want to be good at it."

Name:
Tony Stewart

Date of Birth:
May 20, 1971

Birthplace:
Rushville, Indiana

Resides:
Lake Norman, North Carolina and Columbus, Indiana

Height:
5 ft. 9 in.

Weight:
165 pounds

Marital Status:
Single

Hobbies:
Racing, boating, bowling, and shooting pool

Personal Vehicles:
GMC "Dually," Harley-Davidson "Fat Boy" motorcycle, BMW 540i

Favorite Athlete:
Michael Jordan

Favorite Actor:
Samuel L. Jackson

Favorite Actress:
Crystal Bernard

Favorite Music:
Rock, blues, and country